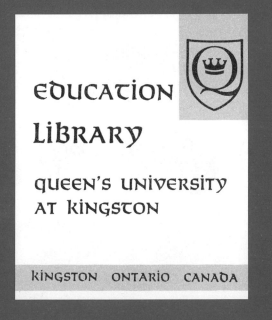

Walrus

Walrus
ON LOCATION

KATHY DARLING
PHOTOGRAPHS BY TARA DARLING

LOTHROP, LEE & SHEPARD BOOKS   NEW YORK

We would like to thank Dr. Francis Fay of the Institute of Marine Science, University of Alaska, Fairbanks, for reading this manuscript for factual accuracy and for sharing walrus knowledge gathered over the past forty years.

Library of Congress Cataloging in Publication Data
Darling, Kathy. Walrus / by Kathy Darling; photographs by Tara Darling.   p.   cm. — (On location)
Summary: Describes the physical characteristics, behavior, eating habits, and predators of the walrus. ISBN 0-688-09032-X. — ISBN 0-688-09033-8 (lib. bdg.) 1. Walruses—Juvenile literature. [1. Walruses.] I. Darling, Tara, ill. II. Title. III. Series: Darling, Kathy. On location.
QL737.P62D37 1991 599.74'7—dc20 90-33376 CIP AC

Contents

Piles of pinnipeds. The walrus is a member of the "fin-footed," or pinniped, family, which includes seals and sea lions.

The Ugli Place

There is an island in Alaska known as the *ugli* place. Each spring, as soon as the ice melts, thousands of walrus gather there to lie in the sun. Round Island's rocky beaches are covered with sunbathing walrus, all grunting and snorting like big, pink pigs. They smell like pigs too—only a lot stinkier! Imagine a beach with twenty thousand pounds of smelly walrus lying in gigantic heaps. These walrus mountains are formed because the big bulls keep climbing out of the icy sea, even when there is no room on the beach. They crawl onto one another—pushing, shoving, and squeezing their fat bodies into every inch of *ugli* space.

Ugli (OOG-ly) is an Eskimo word. It means a place where walrus "haul out," or come ashore. Walrus are so well adapted to life in the water that they can even sleep there. It is hard to imagine why walrus, so strong and swift in the water and so slow and clumsy on land, choose to come out of the water at all. In the high arctic, a place of bitter cold, darkness, and shifting ice, walrus not only survive, they thrive. The arctic sea, with a temperature below the freezing point of fresh water, is where they spend half of their time. On the muddy bottom, they find food. And in the black depths below the ice floes, they mate.

The sea is a good home, but there are several reasons why walrus must leave it. One is safety. Walrus have big, power-

ful enemies, so for protection they form herds. These herds, ranging from ten to two thousand members, are either all-cow-and-young or all-bull groups—except in January and February, which is mating time. It is safer for a herd to sleep on a haul-out than in the water, where currents might separate the animals.

Cow walrus haul out onto ice floes to have their calves. Then they form "nursery herds" made up of cows and newborn calves. Although they can swim from the minute of birth, the calves chill quickly in the icy waters. They have a thick coat of short hair, but it is many weeks before they have enough blubber to stay warm in the water.

Bull herds haul out onto *ugli* beaches after the mating season to heal fighting wounds. Healing is speedier on land. There, the blood necessary to mend the wounds can be supplied to the skin. In the water, blood must be pulled away from the skin in order for the walrus to stay insulated.

Walrus shed their hair every summer

Even from 1,200 feet up, it is easy to spot the red walrus on the rocky, narrow beaches of Round Island.

This walrus must face a ring a tusks as he climbs out of the sea to find a resting place.

and replace it with a new coat in a process called molting. For the month this takes, the haul-out grounds are crowded with hairless walrus that try to stay out of the cold water as much as possible.

Once, there were many *ugli* places. The giant sea mammals never lived in antarctic regions, but fossils show that in ancient times they were numerous along both coasts of North America. They ranged as far south as Georgia on the Atlantic coast and California on the Pacific. During the last three centuries they were hunted everywhere and killed for their ivory tusks, for meat, and for oil. By 1950 the population had dropped from half a million to fifty thousand. The habit of crowding together on an *ugli* was one reason for the decline. It was easy for humans with guns to wipe out whole herds as they slept. One by one, the traditional *ugli* places were abandoned. All the walrus were killed or forced into the high arctic, the only place where man couldn't easily follow. By 1960, things were really tough for walrus. Only one of the old *ugli* places was left in the United States—Round Island.

Three miles long and one mile wide, Round Island is not really round. Its beaches are rocky and narrow. Wind-swept cliffs rise twelve hundred feet, and nothing taller than grass grows on its steep slopes. The sea around it is rough and close to freezing. To most people, Round Island sounds like a terrible place for a summer home. But to a walrus, this *ugli* is beautiful.

Now it is safe, too. In 1960, Round Island and the six islands near it became the Walrus Islands Sanctuary. Because there are people who care about saving the walrus, this last regularly used *ugli* is a protected place, with rangers to guard the herds as they snooze on the beaches.

Dark areas on the bull with the broken tooth show that he has not completed molting. The animal in the background has stab wounds on his face and neck.

For most of the year, walrus are nomads, crisscrossing the vast, shallow arctic seas, and they must have protection *throughout* their range. To determine the needs of the 200,000 members of the species, scientists need to map their movements along the edges of the polar ice cap. This is not as easy as it sounds. Walrus are perfectly suited to subzero temperatures, almost constant darkness, and the continually moving ice pack. But because human beings are not, winter study is difficult. Research during the rest of the year is difficult also. Violent storms interfere with both aerial and shipboard observations. And as if the arctic didn't present enough danger, there are the walrus themselves— huge, powerful meat-eaters! Tara and I had planned to swim with wild walrus and photograph them underwater. But we changed our minds when we learned that walrus sometimes kill and eat small whales and seals. We thought we looked suspiciously like seals in our diving suits!

Because walrus are hunted everywhere but on Round Island, they are afraid of

Radio transmitters, like the one on this bull's tusk, are used to track walrus.

humans. It is only at this special place that close-up walrus watching is possible. So it was here that Tara and I went to study and photograph the giants of the arctic seas. What we learned *On Location* will tell you much about the ways of the walrus, but you will not see ice and snow in these photos because walrus come to Round Island only in the summer. And you will not see pictures of cows or calves because Round Island is used only by bulls. Most of walrus life is a mystery. No one has ever seen a wild walrus eat or mate. No one has ever followed a herd on its long yearly migration. These great discoveries wait for future scientists.

A bull in his prime has tusks 2½ feet long and skin armor called tubercles.

The Tooth-Walkers

Tusks! That's what you first notice when you look at a walrus. And that's the first thing a walrus notices about another walrus. The long upper canine teeth are status symbols in walrus society. They grow throughout the walrus's life, but in old age the growth slows and the tusks begin to wear away. This means a bull walrus in his fighting prime has the biggest tusks. Since all walrus know this, a big tusker can gain respect just by showing off his teeth.

If a walrus wants something more than respect—a choice spot on the beach, for instance—he roars and makes stabbing motions in the air. Usually there is no fight: the walrus with smaller tusks gives in and the prime bull takes what he wants. Tusk displays are definitely not empty threats. Walrus are prepared to back them up with action in the form of a fight. Every day there are lots of little fights. And a few big ones. Most are bloody. Some are even deadly. Quarreling is a way of life in walrus herds.

Sometimes dueling bulls trample other walrus on a crowded beach. The trampled ones strike back at anything within tusk's reach. We once saw thirty jabbing, stabbing walrus. The beach was red with blood.

The walrus's one-inch skin, fifty times thicker than our skin, is as thick as that of

a rhinoceros and just as tough. Mature bulls, which fight more often than other walrus, can be identified by the rough, hairless skin on the neck and shoulders. The lumpy bumps are called tubercles, and they provide another inch of skin armor for mating-age bulls. Females and young animals do not have tubercles. Strangely, neither do captive bulls.

Other than man, the walrus has only two natural enemies—the polar bear and the killer whale. Alone or in a group, walrus will attack a polar bear if they catch it in the water. They kill the white bears as they do seals and beluga whales: by holding them in their front flippers and stabbing them.

Killer whales are a much more dangerous enemy. They are larger and stronger than walrus and can swim faster. And killer whales hunt in packs. If it is attacked by them, a walrus will defend itself with its tusks. Dead killer whales have been found with broken walrus tusks in them, so the walrus must be successful sometimes.

Jabs and stabs! Fights occur mostly between animals whose tusks are similar in size.

Understandably, walrus race for solid ground when they see killer whales. The best defense against them is probably the walrus's choice of a home. They can live where the whales can't. With their huge tusks and thick skulls, walrus can make and maintain breathing holes in ice far from open water, where whales live. Even in open water, walrus favor areas with bits of broken ice, where it is difficult for a killer whale's sonar to detect them.

Walrus are herd animals; and although they often quarrel among themselves, they quickly form a group defense against an outside enemy. Since walrus can't move fast on land, they head for the sea when attacked by man or bear. In the stampede, it's every walrus for itself! But once they're

Frightened walrus stampede into the sea.

tect them. We did see walrus with broken or missing tusks, but most of the bulls on Round Island had a perfect set.

Scientists can tell many things about walrus from the tusks. Age, for instance. At two years, the tiny tusks begin to show beneath the mustached lips; and at about fifteen years, they can be two and a half feet long. Another way to tell walrus age is to count the growth rings on the tusks. Their shape gives researchers a clue to where the walrus lives. There are two varieties, or subspecies, of walrus. Round Island walrus are Pacific walrus. The other kind, the Atlantic walrus, is so threatened it has been put on the endangered-species list. The two varieties look much alike; but the Pacific walrus is heavier, with longer, bigger tusks and a broader muzzle. It is even possible to tell the sex of a walrus by looking at its ivory. The cows have tusks too, but both Atlantic and Pacific females have shorter, slimmer tusks that curve more toward the chest than the males'.

For many years it was thought that the walrus used its tusks to dig clams from the sea bottom. Then walrus researchers noticed that walrus with one or both tusks missing were just as fat and healthy as those with an undamaged set. To find out whether tusks were used in food gathering, scientists buried live clams on the sand bottom of an aquarium and watched how captive walrus uncovered them. It was just as they had suspected. No tusks, no flippers—all the action was in the lips! So, surprisingly, walrus *don't* use their giant teeth as shovels.

Young animals can be identified by their smooth skin and very small tusks.

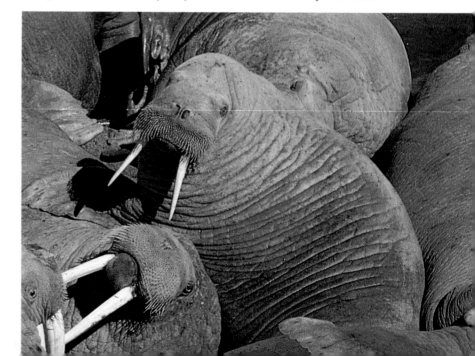

Walrus land on their sides or backs in the shallow water rather than risk damaging their tusks.

They can break even heavier ice with their sharp tusks.

A walrus sometimes uses its tusks as an anchor, hooking them on the edge of a breathing hole when the ice is too thin to haul out onto. The tusk anchor keeps a sleeping walrus from drifting away from its breathing place or from the herd.

Walrus seem to know how important their big white teeth are and carefully proin the water, the walrus join forces and face the danger together, showing the enemy a ring of tusks!

Tusks are used for much more than fighting. A walrus can dig the big ivory teeth into the ice to help pull itself out of the water. It then relies on its tusks and the hard, rough surface of its flippers to pull itself across broken or slippery places on the ice. This behavior gave the walrus its scientific name, *Odobenus*, which means tooth-walker.

The most important use of the tusks may be to chop breathing holes in the ice. If a feeding walrus can't find a hole when it surfaces, it strikes the ice with its head. Walrus are such "hardheads" that their skulls open ice nine inches thick.

Once they are in the water, they turn toward shore and face danger as a group.

The Cliff-Hanger

We were watching puffins, a kind of sea-bird that nests on Round Island, when we heard a walrus grunt. Below us was a big bull and he was in trouble. From our lookout on the cliff, we could see his problem. While he slept, the tide had gone out. On Round Island there is a big tidal drop, and the walrus was stranded on a pile of rocks thirty feet above the water.

The bull moved all around his high prison, looking for a way out. There was no way to the sea except straight down. For an hour he kept roaring and looking over the edge. Then he gathered up his courage and tried to climb down. Going headfirst was too scary, so he decided to go tail first. He lowered his body over the side and tried to reach a ledge with his rear flippers. It was no use. He was up too high. There he was, hanging over the edge of the rocks, holding on with only his front flippers. It looked so hopeless, we could hardly believe what we saw him do next. Balancing on his front flippers, the bull lifted his two-ton body until it was horizontal, then twisted around till he was back on top of the rocks again.

The bull was on the edge of panic now. He went to the other side of the rocks and chose a different spot to try backing down. Things looked good. Then he slipped. Turning his head to protect his tusks, the

bull fell toward the water. He had chosen a bad place—it was a serious mistake. He hit some sharp rocks, bounced twice, and slid into shallow water. The fall had knocked him unconscious.

He floated facedown in the surf, while a cloud of blood blossomed out around him. Waves smashed his body against the rocky shore again and again. There was no movement but that of the sea.

Tara and I thought he was dead. For twenty minutes we watched him in the wild sea. We felt sad to have seen him die. He had tried so hard. Then, to our great surprise, he began to move. At first all he did was breathe. The cliff-hanger acted dazed, shaking his head and swimming in slow little circles for nearly half an hour. Then he joined up with some other walrus that were heading out to the clam beds to feed.

How had he survived? Although the ancestors of the walrus were land animals, their bodies changed over millions of years to help them live in a water world. One

of those changes made our cliff-hanger drownproof. Unlike us, walrus do not breathe automatically. Marine mammals must remember to breathe. This adaptation prevents them from accidentally letting water into their lungs when they are sleeping or unconscious. Although a walrus cannot drown, it can suffocate. The walrus stores large amounts of oxygen in its blood and muscles, so it can go without breathing for a long time, perhaps for an hour. But when the stored oxygen is used up, the walrus must breathe or die.

The cliff-hanger was bleeding when he hit the water. But in a few seconds his blood had clotted and the wounds had begun to close up. Superfast healing is another marine adaptation. Human blood will not clot in water. We can bleed to death in a few minutes. Walrus have a chemical in their blood that makes it clot in salt water. This mechanism also protects them from predators that might be attracted to the smell of blood.

Go with the Floe

Pacific walrus make one of the longest migrations of any mammal. Following the moving ice pack with the changing seasons, they travel up to two thousand miles every year. The reason for the great journey is food, and it is made possible by ice floes.

Ice floes are floating beds. Walrus can rest far from shore on them, drifting with the ocean currents to a fresh feeding ground while they sleep.

Walrus require a large area in which to feed because their prey is small and slow to reproduce. By using ice floes for transportation, walrus can forage over the entire arctic region.

There may not be as much food around Round Island as there is in the high arctic, where the cows and calves spend the summer; but there is plenty for the bull herd during the few months they spend there. Round Island is a busy place, with small groups of walrus moving between the beaches and the feeding grounds every few minutes. A feeding group usually goes to sea for seven or eight days and then returns to the haul-out, where it sleeps for two or three days.

Walrus never travel alone. There is always danger from killer whales in open water. A hungry walrus enters the water and swims back and forth about one hundred yards off the beach. When another walrus comes out, the two touch

"Exchange breathing" is one way walrus identify each other.

noses and do what is called exchange breathing. By inhaling the air that the other animal has just exhaled, they identify each other. Then they swim together, waiting for others to join their group. The noisy, snorting breathing, which can be heard from shore, sounds like that of horses. The name *walrus* comes from an old Viking word that means whale horse. Soon, four or five of the "whale horses" have exchanged breath, and the group takes off for the clam beds. Older walrus

This group of walrus is heading for the clam beds. The young one in the middle is about seven years old. This is probably his first year at Round Island.

accompany the young ones, perhaps protecting them and showing them the best places to find food.

The walrus is a benthos, or bottom, feeder. It roots along the muddy floor of the sea in search of clams, snails, worms, and crabs. Clams are the favored food. And it takes lots and lots of clams to feed a hungry walrus. Most of a walrus's time is spent gathering the 800 giant clams, 10,000 small clams, or 100 pounds of mixed worms that it needs every day. Averaging 7 or 8 minutes per dive, a walrus may feed as deep as 300 feet below the surface. To locate its food in the darkness of the ocean floor, the walrus uses very sensitive whiskers called *vibrissae*.

When it finds a tasty clam, the walrus squirts a jet of water from its mouth and uncovers the morsel. Then it purses its thick lips around it and literally sucks the clam right out of the shell. Although the walrus has many teeth, it does not chew its food. It swallows it live and whole.

Compared to a seal, a walrus is a slow swimmer. Since it doesn't catch moving

A walrus cannot smell under water. He uses his mustache, made up of 700 sensitive hairs called vibrissae, to find food.

prey, as the fish-eating seals do, there is no need to swim fast. Only the hind flippers are used in swimming. The big, webbed rear flippers are stroked to the side one at a time. The toes are spread on

Walrus are long-distance swimmers. They can swim hundreds of miles without going ashore to rest.

the outward stroke for maximum power and are pressed together on the return stroke. The front flippers are held against the body and are used mainly for steering. On land the walrus walks on all four feet.

Walrus can swim at five miles an hour for hundreds of miles without stopping. On the long migration, they cover most of the distance by swimming; but they spend some of the time drifting on ice floes that pass over the clam beds. On the ice is where the walrus want to be. Given a choice between ice and land for a resting place, walrus choose to "go with the floe."

Out in the Cold

It was a beautiful midsummer day on Round Island. The sun was bright, but the temperature was only a little above freezing. Tara and I huddled in our coats and tried to keep out of the wind as we set up the cameras. The big bulls were quiet, sleeping peacefully in the sun for a change. Most of them were upside down, with their flippers in the air. They weren't trying to warm up, they were trying to cool off.

A walrus is so well insulated that it can overheat when the temperature is 0° Fahrenheit. The walrus's insulating system, designed to withstand arctic seas, which conduct heat away from the body twenty times faster than air, is a sort of three-layer parka: hair on the outside, inch-thick skin, and special insulating fat called blubber.

The 98° F temperature of a walrus is about the same as that of a human. To maintain this temperature in the sea, blood is pumped away from the skin, into the muscles and inner body core, which are insulated by the blubber. Seawater can drop *below* freezing in the arctic, but the skin temperature of a walrus can safely drop to that of the surrounding water. There might be more than 100° F difference between the internal and external temperatures of a swimming walrus. Internal parts are still toasty warm when the skin is so cold that falling snow does not melt on it. When a walrus comes out of cold water, the nearly bloodless skin is a ghostly white. After a while in the sun, the blood returns and the walrus turns pink, then bright rust red. Sometimes, it is all these colors at once—a living patchwork quilt.

Red walrus are walrus trying to keep their cool. The red color shows that their bodies are trying to get rid of excess heat by sending blood into the skin, where it can cool off. An upside-down position exposes the flippers, which have blood vessels close to the surface, to cooling breezes.

Heat control in the flippers is different from that in the rest of the body. Flippers have no hair and almost no blubber to insulate the muscles. If the muscles were deprived of blood, as the skin is, the walrus wouldn't be able to walk or swim. But having warm blood flowing through the flippers would lead to enormous heat loss in the cold water, a loss the walrus couldn't tolerate. Further, warm flippers would melt the ice around them, which could refreeze and trap the walrus. (If your hand has ever stuck to an ice-cube tray, you have

This overheated bull is trying to reduce his temperature by waving his flippers in the air.

One or two hours after he emerges from the water, this ghostly bull will turn the same rust color as his brothers on the beach.

witnessed a version of this phenomenon.) The walrus don't have to deal with it, though—they have cold feet!

The walrus has a simple but clever arrangement of veins and arteries that keeps the flippers cool while still providing an adequate blood supply. This system, known as the "wonderful net," is located where the flippers join the body. The arteries bringing warm blood from the heart are surrounded by the veins returning cold blood from the flippers. Heat escaping from the arteries warms the returning blood in the nearby veins. In that way the heat isn't wasted, but is saved and used to maintain the walrus's body temperature. Just enough heat is left in the blood flowing to the flippers to keep them functional. So far as is known, the walrus feels no discomfort in its cold flippers and the muscles don't lose mobility as human muscles do in the cold.

The size of the walrus is another adaptation that conserves body heat. Round Island bulls reach an awesome two tons. When it comes to survival in the heat-draining seas, nature favors "blimps" like the walrus. A big animal loses heat much more slowly than a small one. A small body, even if it were very fat, wouldn't be efficient. The Pacific walrus, one of the largest animals on earth and the biggest year-round resident of the arctic, is the model of efficiency.

This bull's skin looks like a patchwork quilt.

A fat walrus is a healthy walrus. Three-inch-thick blubber on this two-ton animal keeps him warm in the arctic seas.

Walrus Songs

In the quiet of the midnight sun when the wind dies down, the walrus go for a promenade round the island they share with 450,000 seabirds, foxes, mice, and a herd of sea lions. They all swim leisurely in the same direction, in groups of four or five, doing laps, sometimes stopping to make the strange music called belling. Haunting and beautiful, it sounds like cathedral chimes. It is a walrus love song.

Young males spend many hours practicing these mating songs, which they will later need to attract females. The songs are not sung in their normal barking voice. Bull walrus have a throat sac that they inflate to make the bell sound. The melodies, which we could hear on the cliffs of Round Island, are sung underwater. They usually begin with a series of knocking sounds, followed by clear bell tones. The belling bounces off flat underwater rocks, producing a song that can be heard almost a mile away. The young singer finishes by sticking his head out of the water, making a clicking noise, smacking his lips, and looking around to see if anyone nearby is impressed by his song.

The "singing sac" has another use. When it is inflated, the walrus floats upright. Bulls sleep at sea in this fashion. Cows do not have throat sacs. Instead, they blow up their lungs like balloons when

A singing walrus. The inflated throat sac shows that he is belling.

The singer in the water has an audience on the rocks.

they need to sleep at sea. Although they do not float "standing up" with their faces above water as the bulls do, they are close to the surface and merely have to lift their nostrils to breathe.

Only Pacific walrus sing in American waters. They sing the song of a species 200,000 strong; but without protection all the singers could be silenced. There are those who would kill every last walrus for the ivory tusks. The Atlantic walrus is already extinct in much of its former range, and the small, scattered populations that have managed to survive are all threatened. Their numbers are down to about 20,000 and are not increasing.

Walrus are big, ugly, and dangerous—yet we must care that they are disappearing. All living things, including humans, are connected in a fragile, delicately balanced web of life. When we disturb that balance, we do not know what will happen. To keep the planet healthy for humans, we must also keep it healthy for walrus.

Trying to preserve the balance of life is a great challenge, and you can help. It is never too early or too late to work for something that really matters.

And walrus, like all living things, matter. The song of life should include a choir of walrus singers, belling love songs into the arctic sea.

The Migration of the Pacific Walrus

Maximum concentrations of walrus are shown darker

Spring: The herds split into all-male and all-female-and-young groups. Most of the adult bulls go to Round Island in Alaska or to islands off Siberia. Females continue north to the rich feeding grounds of the Chukchi Sea, joining the migration of seals, whales, dolphins, and seabirds through the narrow Bering Strait in May. Babies are born during the migration, usually in May. Cows and calves reach their destination in June or July.

Fall: In September the females and calves begin to move south, timing their journey so they get through the Bering Strait before the December freeze-up. Bulls leave their summering grounds in October and swim north to join the females. When they arrive at the wintering grounds, the females may have traveled 2,000 miles and the males may have covered 1,500 miles.

Summer: Females, babies, and juveniles feed in the Chukchi Sea. Males remain on *ugli* beaches and feed in the Bering Sea.

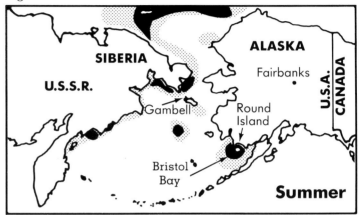

Winter: Mixed herds of males and females gather on ice floes in the Bering Sea. Mating takes place in January and February, well within the southward-moving pack ice. The ice reaches its southernmost point in March or April.

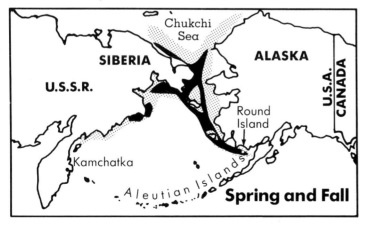

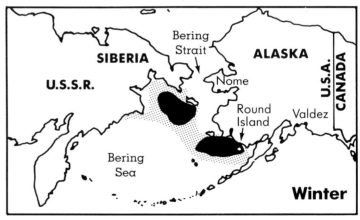

Walrus Facts

Common Name: Walrus. Subspecies: Pacific walrus, Atlantic walrus. Male: bull. Female: cow. Baby: calf. Group: herd.

Scientific Name: Odobenus rosmarus. This means "tooth-walking horse of the sea."

Related Species: Seals and sea lions.

Size: Male: 9 to 12 feet long; 2,000 to 4,000 pounds. Female: 7½ to 10 feet long; 900 to 2,700 pounds.

Color: Reddish brown.

Food: Carnivorous. Eats 75–100 pounds of meat a day from ocean floor. Mostly clams, crabs, snails, and worms. Occasionally eats seals.

Habitat/Range: Northern polar regions. Prefers pack ice above water 30 to 300 feet deep.

Life Span: Maximum 40 years.

Sexual Maturity: Male: 15 years. Female: 8 years.

Gestation: One calf after 15-month pregnancy. Females produce a calf every 2 to 4 years.

Population: Estimated 250,000 Pacific walrus and 20,000 Atlantic walrus.

Predators: Humans, killer whales, and polar bears.

Behavior: Herd forming. Nomadic. Aggressive. Spends about half of time in water and half hauled out on ice floes or beaches.

Index